JAMES

LECTIO DIVINA FOR YOUTH

JAMES

LECTIO DIVINA FOR YOUTH

ANCIENT FAITH SERIES

Barefoot Ministries®
Kansas City, Missouri

Written by Alex Varughese

Editor: Mike Wonch
Assistant Editor: Catherine M. Shaffer
Cover Design: JR Caines
Interior Design: Sharon Page

Adapted from *Lectio Divina Bible Studies: Listening for God Through James*.

Varughese, Alex. *Lectio Divina Bible Studies: Listening for God Through James*. Indianapolis, IN: Wesleyan Publishing House and Beacon Hill Press of Kansas City, 2006.

Library of Congress Cataloging-in-Publication Data : 2009908229

10 9 8 7 6 5 4 3 2 1

ABOUT THE
LECTIO DIVINA
BIBLE STUDIES

Lectio divina (pronounced lek-tsee-oh dih-vee-nuh), is a Latin phrase that means *sacred reading.* It is the ancient Christian practice of communicating with God through the reading and study of Scripture. Throughout history, great Christian leaders have used and adapted this ancient method of interpreting Scripture.

The idea behind *lectio divina* is to look at a Bible passage in such a way that Bible study becomes less about study and more about listening. The approach is designed to focus our attention on what God is saying to us through the Word. Through the process of *lectio divina* we not only read to understand with our minds, but we read to hear with our hearts and obey. It is a way of listening to God through His Word.

Some throughout history have said that *lectio divina* turns Bible study on its head—normally we read the Bible, but in *lectio divina, the Bible reads us.* That is probably a good way to describe it. It is God using His Word in a conversation with us to read into our lives and speak to our hearts.

In this series, we will use the traditional *lectio divina* model. We have expanded each component so that it can be used by both individuals and by groups. Each session in this study includes the following elements. (Latin words and their pronunciation are noted in parentheses.)

- **Reading** (*Lectio* "lek-tsee-oh"). We begin with a time of quieting ourselves prior to reading. Then we take a slow, careful reading of a passage of Scripture. We focus our minds on the central theme of the passage. When helpful, we read out loud or read the same passage over and over several times.

- **Meditation** (*Meditatio* "medi-tah-tsee-oh"). Next, we explore the meaning of the Bible passage. Here we dig deep to try to understand all of what God might be saying to us. We think on the passage. We explore the images, and pay attention to the emotions and feelings that the passage provides. We put ourselves in the story. We look for particular words or phrases that leap off the page as the Spirit begins to speak to us through the Word.

- **Prayer** (*Oratio* "or-ah-tsee-oh"). As we meditate on the passage, we respond to God by communicating with Him. We specifically ask God to speak to us through His Word. We begin to dialog with Him about what we have read. We express praise, thanksgiving, confession, or agreement to God. And we listen. We wait before Him in silence, allowing God the chance to speak.

- **Contemplation** (*Contemplatio* "con-tehm-plah-tsee-oh"). At this point in our conversation through the Word, we come to a place where we rest in the presence of God. Our study is now about receiving what He has said to us. Imagine two old friends who have just talked at length—and now without words, they just sit together and enjoy each other's presence. Having spent time listening to God, we know a little better how God is shaping the direction of our lives. Here there is a yielding of oneself to God's will. We resolve to act on the message of Scripture.

GROUP STUDY

This book is designed to be useful for both individual and group study. To use this in a group, you may take one of several approaches:

- **Individual Study/Group Review**. Make sure each member of the group has a copy of the book. Have them read through one section during the week. (They will work through the same passage or portions of it each day that week.) Then, when you meet together, review what thoughts, notes, and insights the members of the group experienced in their individual study. Use the group questions at the end of the section as a guide.

- **Group Lectio**. Make sure each member of the group has a copy of the book. Have them read through one section during the week in individual study. When you meet together as a group, you will study the passage together through a reading form similar to lectio divina:

- ○ **First, read the passage out loud several times to the group**. Group members respond by waiting in silence and letting God speak.
- ○ **Second, have the passage read aloud again to the group once or twice more**. Use different group members for different voices, and have them read slowly. Group members listen for a word or two that speaks to them, and share it with the group. Break into smaller groups if appropriate.
- ○ **Third, read the passage out loud again, and have the group pray together to ask God what He might be saying to each person, and to the group as a whole**. Go around and share what each person is learning from this process. At this point, review together the group questions at the end of the section.[1]
- • **Lectio Divina Steps for Groups**. Make sure each member has a copy of the book. As a group, move through the study together, going through each of the parts: reading, mediation, prayer, and contemplation. Be sure to use the group questions at the end of the section.

The important thing about using *lectio divina* in a group is to remember that this is to be incarnational ("in the flesh")—in other words, we begin to live out the Word in our community. We carry God's Word in us, (in the flesh, or incarnate in us) and we carry that Word into our group to be lived out among them.

The *Lectio Divina Bible Studies* invite readers to slow down, read Scripture, meditate upon it, and prayerfully respond to God's Word.

---

1. Parts of the "Group Lectio" section adapted from Tony Jones, *The Sacred Way: Spiritual Practices for Everyday Life*, Grand Rapids: Zondervan, 2005, p. 54.

CONTENTS

INTRODUCTION

Imagine if you had grown up in the shadow of your perfect half-brother Jesus. What would you have learned watching the God-man experience life a few years ahead of you? What would you have felt as He spoke to the crowds, raised the dead, healed the sick, and fed thousands with a little boy's lunch? What about as you watched public opinion turn against Him or as you watched Him die?

James, the author of this book, experienced these things. During Jesus' public ministry, younger brother James seems to have been a doubter (John 7:5). Yet the resurrected Christ appeared especially to this brother (1 Cor. 15:7), and James was among the believers as they gathered in the Upper Room in Acts 2. At some point, James became a true spiritual brother of his earthly brother.

After Peter's angelic deliverance from a Jerusalem jail, James assumed leadership of the Jerusalem church. His Epistle may have been the first New Testament book written, as early as A.D. 45, a date before the apostle Paul's ministry and before the influx of Gentiles into the church.

In style and tone, James often sounds much like Jesus. Compare, for example, James 1:12 with Jesus' words in Matthew 5:11-12. James uses Greek with ease, yet demonstrates an up-close knowledge of Jewish law. Some scholars speculate that the book may have originated as a collection of sermons.

Its content is focused on the practical, day-to-day following of the example of Jesus, in word and in deed. One key theme is that the little sins we consider more acceptable (like gossip, jealousy, favoritism, and hoarding wealth) are as ugly in God's eyes as the biggies. This book also contains powerful challenges to stand firm in difficulty and to cultivate a fervent life of prayer. Its instructions have everything to do with how true believers—then and now—live as Christ-followers in the real world.

THE ROAD TO CHRISTIAN MATURITY
LISTENING FOR GOD THROUGH JAMES 1:1-12

SUMMARY

The road to Christian maturity is not an easy path. It takes us through the difficult and unpleasant experiences of our human existence. Some of these experiences may be daily struggles of life shared by all humanity, but other experiences go beyond the ordinary, and these we may find difficult and even unbearable. Regardless of the size of our struggles, we have the choice to allow them to hinder us or help us in our spiritual growth. The outcome depends on the way we encounter trials.

Trials of life, if encountered with uncertainty and wavering, will result in a defeated Christian life. This option will take us nowhere. Trials of life, if encountered with commitment and trust in God, will foster spiritual growth. This second road leads to a deep, satisfying life. James helps us discover this road to Christian maturity through today's reading.

PREPARATION ✝ FOCUS YOUR THOUGHTS

How do you respond to the struggles of life? What is the level of your perseverance?

When you pray, do you pray with confidence that God will answer your prayer, or do you pray with uncertainty about God's answer?

READING ✝ HEAR THE WORD

James the Just, brother of Jesus, applies in this letter the foundational teachings of Jesus to specific situations that his audience faced in the middle of the first century. The suffering of the Christian community is a key concern in this book of the Bible. James's goal is to challenge his audience to persevere in the midst of trials and to stand firm in their trust in God.

In this opening section, you will encounter the following words and phrases:

> *Servant:* Though a leader, James sees himself as a slave called into the service of God.
> *The 12 tribes of Israel:* James uses this term to describe believers.
> *Pure joy:* A joy that is deep and overflowing.
> *Trials:* The experience of suffering and hardship in life.
> *Perseverance:* A firm, consistent display of faith and commitment.

Wisdom: A gift from God that gives a person the ability to discern God's plans.

Believe: The commitment to trust God.

Doubt: Wavering thoughts and actions despite a knowledge of the truth.

Crown of life: Eternal life.

Look for these phrases as you read James 1:1-12.

MEDITATION ☦ ENGAGE THE WORD

Meditate on James 1:1-4

James calls his readers to have deep and overflowing joy when they face difficult situations in life. He reminds them that perseverance is necessary for their development as whole persons. What kind of trials does James refer to? Why does James think it is possible for a believer to have deep joy in the midst of life's adversities?

Read the verse below from Paul's letter to the Philippians. What do you think was the source of Paul's rejoicing? Why did he challenge his readers to always rejoice? How difficult is it to rejoice in light of the trials James mentions? Why?

> Rejoice in the Lord always. I will say it again: Rejoice!
> —Paul (Phil. 4:4)

Perseverance is a rare character trait in our day. Why do most people lack this character trait?

James indicates that perseverance is a process—a character trait developed over time. How can perseverance be developed in the life of a Christian according to James?

According to verse 4, we are to lack nothing. What do you lack in your life? What do you need to do to gain what is lacking in your life?

Meditate on James 1:5-8

James reminds his readers that they should ask God for wisdom to withstand trials. Wisdom is a true display of the generosity of God. It is a gift wrapped with the presence of the Holy Spirit who comforts and sustains the people of God in their trials. When faced with trials, what does your first response tend to be?

James challenges his readers to ask for wisdom from God with an unwavering attitude. What do you think James meant by "he must believe?" What is the difference between honest doubt and doubt that is a hindrance to faith?

Read the quote from F. Mussner on page 17 and reflect on the root cause of a person's inner conflict between the trust and distrust of God. Now reflect on a time or an event when you had the greatest difficulty trusting God. How did you overcome that situation?

> The doubter is "one who lives in inner conflict between
> trust and distrust of God." —F. Mussner,
> quoted by Peter H. Davids

Meditate on James 1:9-11

James speaks about the poor and the rich. The present condition of the poor is deplorable, whereas the present condition of the rich is comfortable. Why do you think James speaks of the poor and the rich in this text? How do these verses relate to the preceding verses?

Read the quote from Jesus. Then read its context, Luke 18:18-25. Think about James's statement in light of the story of the rich ruler in Luke's Gospel.

> How hard it is for the rich to enter the kingdom of
> God! —Jesus (Luke 18:24)

Those who are preoccupied with their present circumstances may never truly know the joy that lies ahead. Yet the road to maturity invites us to have a broader perspective. What are the things you are preoccupied with these days? How do you see yourself? Are you poor or rich from God's perspective?

Meditate on James 1:12

God promises His children that perseverance through trials leads to the reward of eternal life. James's words here are a pronouncement of blessing and an invitation to those who become bogged down by the pressures of life and give up too quickly. What do you see as James's invitation to you in this verse? How would you explain the promise in this verse to someone who is struggling to maintain faith?

PRAYER ☦ ASK AND LISTEN

Seek the face of God. Ask, "Lord, what are You saying to us today?"

James invites Christians to receive God's gift of wisdom—the Holy Spirit—to help us withstand the trials of life. Pray silently for God's gift. Pray with the certainty that God not only hears, but will answer your prayer.

CONTEMPLATION ☦ REFLECT AND YIELD

How would your life be different if you were totally committed to trusting God in the middle of trials?

Do you see the present realities of your life with the broader perspective of God's will and purpose for your life? Are you open to the gift God has for you?

GROUP STUDY

- What do you think is the true measure of a mature Christian?

- How do you handle the trials of life?

- Has there been a time when you tried to handle a trial on your own strength? If so, what happened?

- Has there been a time when you asked the Holy Spirit to help you during a trial? If so, what happened?

- What lessons have you learned from each of those experiences?

- What are the keys to persevering during the trials of life?

- God calls us not only to trust in Him but to lead others into a trusting relationship with Him. Think of someone you know who is easily dragged down by the struggles of life. Make a commitment to seek out that person and help him or her develop a stronger faith in God.

LIVING IN THE WORD
LISTENING FOR GOD THROUGH JAMES 1:13-27

SUMMARY

True Christian life is lived in the Word. Those who live in the Word know that God does not tempt His people. Rather, He teaches them to avoid temptations. God's children, born through His truth, should live lives of self-control and practice discipline in speech and action.

For James, the key to this new birth and new way of life is being a hearer and doer of God's revealed Word. He calls us not only to hear the Word, but to follow it with action. Those who live in the Word practice true faith: a life of compassion for the poor in the world. This goes way beyond empty rituals.

In this section of James, you will discover the qualities of a life that is lived in the Word of God.

PREPARATION ☦ FOCUS YOUR THOUGHTS

If you could choose a particular way of life, what would it be? Why would you make that choice? How different is that way of life from the way you live now?

READING ☦ HEAR THE WORD

After dealing with the issue of trials and the call to seek God's wisdom to withstand them, James reminds his readers that they should live by the Word through which God has given them life.

In this Scripture passage, you will encounter the following words and phrases:

> *Tempted:* In Greek, this verb shares the same root word with the noun *trial*, but it conveys the added meaning of being enticed to sin.
>
> *Evil desire:* Natural human desires that have been corrupted by sin.
>
> *Perfect law:* The law of love that Jesus taught and practiced.
>
> *Religion:* A human response to God through internal and external forms of worship.
>
> *World (Kosmos in the Greek):* James here refers to the place of human existence that is corrupt and sinful.

Read James 1:13-27, paying special attention to these phrases in context.

MEDITATION ⚱ ENGAGE THE WORD

Meditate on James 1:13-18

Trials offer the opportunity for growth. Yet trials, if misunderstood as temptations sent by God, will lead us to sin. Why do you think James insists on asserting that God does not tempt (test) anyone?

Since temptations originate in one's evil desires, James calls people to take moral responsibility for their actions. Why do people often seek someone or something to blame for their actions? Have you ever given in to the temptation to blame someone else for your sin?

Compare James 1:4 with 1:15. Note that the God who gives us wisdom to withstand trials will not send temptations to mislead or cause us to fall into the trap of sin. How do these verses differ in the messages they communicate? What can you learn from reading them together?

What is the truth claim being made by the MasterCard ad on page 24? Compare it with the truth claim of James about the constancy of God. Why do you think James contrasts God's constancy with the lack of constancy in the sun and moon?

> *In a world of constant changes, one thing remains constant: MasterCard.* —*TV commercial*

How does the Word (Jesus; see John 1:1) work in you to make you God's new creation?

Read the quote from Richard Foster and reflect on how Christ is formed in you. What does it mean to have Christ formed in you? What part do you have in the process?

> *For the Christian heaven is not the goal, it is the destination. The goal is that Christ be formed in you.* —*Richard J. Foster*

Meditate on James 1:19-21

The wisdom of God leads one to develop the disciplines of listening and speaking. Why is it important to listen carefully before we speak? Why is it important to speak cautiously and deliberately, with well-chosen words?

James reminds his readers that humble submission to God's Word is the antidote to the poison of immorality. What does James mean by "humbly accept the word planted in you, which can save you?"

Meditate on James 1:22-25

Knowledge of the Word alone is not sufficient; hearing the Word without putting it into daily action is an act of self-deception. Why is it difficult to do what the Word says? What troubles have you experienced in this area?

For James, obedience is a way of life. What is this passage saying to people who have good intentions to obey God's Word, but often neglect to carry it out? How do the words of verse 25, "being not hearers who forget but doers who act" (NRSV), apply to you?

Meditate on James 1:26-27

James connects true religion with living an ethical life characterized by disciplined speech, works of charity, service to the poor, and a total rejection of the evil influences of the world. How do these characteristics play out in your daily life? In what areas do you think God would have you improve? What words would you use to describe your Christian life?

What does James mean when he concludes this section by reminding us to keep a "tight rein" on our tongues? What would others say about your speech?

Read and reflect on the words of Mother Teresa on page 26, a saintly woman of few words but great actions. How would your life change if you were to apply her words to your actions?

We are supposed to preach without preaching not by
words, but by our examples, by our actions.

—*Mother Teresa*

PRAYER ♱ ASK AND LISTEN

Seek the face of God. Ask, "Lord, what are You saying to us today?"

Living in the Word means being firmly planted in biblical truth. What is your present relationship to the Word? What are the influences of this world that keep you from faithfully living in the Word?

Pray silently and seek God's wisdom to say no to the temptations that come your way.

CONTEMPLATION ♱ REFLECT AND YIELD

What are the benefits and blessings of a life lived in the Word? How would your life be changed if you became a person committed to ethical living through careful speech and compassionate deeds?

GROUP STUDY

- How do you respond to temptation?

- What are the areas of temptation to which you are most vulnerable?

- Based on James 1:14-15, what can we do to make sure we do not give in to temptations?

- Think of a person whom you have offended by angry words. Share with that person what God is saying to you and ask for forgiveness.

- Think of a time when you have been quick to speak and slow to listen. What was the outcome?

- Now think of a time when you listened well and spoke few words. What was the outcome then?

- Think of a person who is among the neglected people in the world. Decide on at least one thing you will do to bring a blessing to that person.

KEEPING THE ROYAL LAW
LISTENING FOR GOD THROUGH JAMES 2:1-13

SUMMARY

God created all humanity in His image; all are equal in His sight. In our worldly perspective, we see the rich and the poor, the black and the white, the good looking and the not-so-good looking, the educated and the illiterate. The outcome of drawing such lines is the preferential treatment of one group at the expense of the other.

James saw favoritism as a critical problem in the Christian community of his day. In particular, he was uncomfortable with preferential treatment of the rich at the expense of the poor. He says favoritism among God's people is a violation of God's command to love your neighbor as yourself. Breaking this commandment means breaking all of God's commandments.

What does it really mean to love your neighbor? Who do you consider your neighbor? Who does God consider your neighbor?

PREPARATION ✞ FOCUS YOUR THOUGHTS

What is your attitude toward wealth and poverty? What are your fears, if you are wealthy? What are your concerns, if you are poor?

READING ✞ HEAR THE WORD

In this chapter, James moves into another area of ethical living. He is concerned about those who call themselves Christians but practice discrimination against the poor. Ethical living calls for equal treatment of all regardless of economic or social status.

In this Scripture, you will encounter the following terms:

> *Poor:* This term defined the identity of a Christian in the Early Church.
> *Your meeting:* A gathering of the Christians. James uses the Greek term for synagogue, rather than *ekklesia*, the common term for church.
> *Kingdom:* God's offer of salvation to the poor.
> *The rich:* This term referred to those outside the Christian community.

The royal law: This term refers to Jesus' explicit commandment to "love your neighbor as yourself."

Mercy: A broad term that encompasses meeting the needs of others.

Consider how each of these terms applies to your own life as you read James 2:1-13.

MEDITATION ✝ ENGAGE THE WORD

Meditate on James 2:1-7

James calls on Christians to practice equal treatment of all who come to worship. Showing favoritism to those who are wealthy and treating the poor as second-class citizens indicates the practice of prejudice in the Church. How is prejudice still an issue in the Church today? How about in your own faith practice?

Why do you think James was concerned about the issue of favoritism? What is he saying to the church of his day that struggled with this issue?

How does James's statement about favoritism relate to a local church where the wealth/poverty difference is not as apparent? What are the indications of favoritism in the Church today?

Read the quote by Mother Teresa. Why did she think the poor have so much to give to those who are better off?

> We don't realize the greatness of the poor and how
> much they give us.   —Mother Teresa

What does James mean when he says those who show favoritism have become "judges with evil thoughts?" How does favoritism become an evil act?

According to James, the poor who love God are heirs to His kingdom, and thus they are rich from a spiritual perspective. What is James saying to Christians who may be poor in the eyes of the world today? What is James saying to Christians who may be wealthy in the eyes of the world today?

Compare James 2:5 with Matthew 5:3. See if Jesus' statement helps to offer further understanding of the requirements for one's inheritance of God's kingdom. In what sense are you rich in your present relationship with God? How do you identify with the poor in the world?

Meditate on James 2:8-13

The royal law, "Love your neighbor as yourself" (Lev. 19:18), is a commandment found in a number of places in the New Testament. Why do you think this was an important guideline for early Christians?

Read Proverbs 14:21, and see how James tries to make a connection between the neighbor and the needy. What is the significance of this connection? What does it mean for you personally?

Read the quote by Aristides from the second century A.D. How did Christians show their love for their neighbor? How did these actions make an impact on a watching world? What did they say about Christ through their actions toward orphans and the poor?

> They love one another, and from widows they do not turn away their esteem; and they deliver the orphan from him who treats him harshly . . . And verily, this is a new people, and there is something divine in the midst of them.
>
> —Aristides, a pagan, defending the Christians before Emperor Hadrian

Learning from James and early Christians, whom do you consider as your neighbor? What do you consider as the greatest commandment you follow?

James says breaking one law equals breaking all the laws of God. He also shows that our speech and conduct must be shaped by the conviction that the law that sets us free is also the law that convicts us. What is the law that gives us freedom? What place do you give to the royal law in your life?

Read the quote from Richard Nixon. What does the image of black and white notes mean to you in the context of James's words on favoritism?

> *If you want to make beautiful music, you must play the black and the white notes together.* —Richard Nixon

What connection do you see between 2:3-4 and 2:13? How do you see yourself in light of this Scripture? Can you think of an instance when mercy triumphed over judgment?

PRAYER ✝ ASK AND LISTEN

Seek the face of God. Ask, "Lord, what are You saying to us today?"

The Gospels show that Jesus treated all people alike; in His eyes, there were no rich or poor. We live in a world that is sharply divided by race, socioeconomics, and religious preferences. Pray silently, asking God to help you be like Jesus in this world.

CONTEMPLATION ✝ REFLECT AND YIELD

What would your life be like if you were transformed by the call to show mercy and not favoritism? Are you ready to accept the challenge of James? Are you ready to make a decision to yield completely to the royal law?

GROUP STUDY

- How do you treat the rich? How do you treat the poor? Is there a difference between how you treat the rich and how you treat the poor? If so, why?

- What are some examples of favoritism from our world?

- Why do you think favoritism is so serious that it is considered a sin (verse 9)?

- In what ways can you practice the "royal law" today?

- What is the consequence of judgment without mercy?

- How does "mercy triumph over judgment?"

- In what way will you become an agent of transformation in the Church when you see judgment without mercy?

A LIVING FAITH
LISTENING FOR GOD THROUGH JAMES 2:14-26

SUMMARY

Mother Teresa was invited to participate in a world conference on hunger in Bombay. She arrived at the conference building late because she got lost on the way. As she was going into the building, she saw a man lying in front of the door dying of hunger. She carried the man to the nearest home for the dying and missed the conference entirely. Imagine the irony of the situation. This man lay dying on the doorstep of the very building where representatives from powerful countries were confidently discussing plans to eliminate hunger in the next 15 years.

Are we in the Church more like the compassionate nun or the confident bureaucrats? We will find the answer in our actions, rather than our words. What do we do with our faith? Is it dead or alive? How do we know if our faith is dead or alive? If our faith is dead, how do we bring it to life? James invites us to ponder these questions and transform our dead religion into a living, vibrant faith.

PREPARATION ✝ FOCUS YOUR THOUGHTS

Why do you think others who went to the conference on hunger failed to notice the dying man on the doorstep? Why is it easy to have faith, but difficult to act? What would the world be like if the Church actually lived out the example of Jesus Christ?

READING ✝ HEAR THE WORD

In this section, James uses the literary device of a moral diatribe: a semi-conversational, question-and-implied-answer format that was popular in Greek communications. This device serves to establish his claim that if one has faith, it must be demonstrated through deeds of charity and righteousness.

In this Scripture, you will encounter the following terms:

Faith: The knowledge of the correct doctrine.
Deeds: This term also can be translated as *works*. (See Rom. 11:6.). Paul uses this term to convey works of the Law or legalistic observances, whereas in James, it means good deeds expected of a Christian.
Without clothes: This term refers to the outer garment needed to keep warm at night.

The scripture was fulfilled: This conveys the idea that one biblical text agrees with and supports another part of the Scriptures.

God's friend: The title *friend* for Abraham is found in 2 Chronicles 20:7 and Isaiah 41:8.

Rahab: An Old Testament example of hospitality to strangers. Her story appears in Joshua chapters 2 and 6.

Read James 2:14-26, listening for what God will say to you personally.

MEDITATION ⚜ ENGAGE THE WORD

Meditate on James 2:14-17

James makes the solid claim that the mental acceptance of the beliefs of faith unaccompanied by obedient actions cannot lead to anything good. One can trust in Jesus as Savior, yet if this faith is not put into action, it is not a living faith.

How would you describe James's understanding of salvation? How do faith and deeds go hand-in-hand in the Christian life?

What understanding do you get about discipleship from this text? How would you have responded if you were the person in James's hypothetical example?

Read the quote by Francis Beaumont. How does this analogy apply to the Christian life?

> *Faith without works is like a bird without wings; though she may hop with her companions on earth, yet she will never fly with them to heaven.*
>
> —Francis Beaumont

What do you think James is saying here about the responsibility of the Christian community to those within the community who have physical needs? What would James say to a local Christian community where there may not be any serious physical need?

Some people think Christians should only be concerned with other Christians in need. How would you respond to this attitude?

Meditate on James 2:18-20

James anticipates an objection to his belief that faith without works is dead. Some may think that faith and good deeds are unrelated to each other and that they are two different gifts. He argues that a good deed is the concrete proof of the existence of a faith that is alive. How do you respond to that statement?

In verse 19, James introduces the most basic foundational belief of Judaism: "There is one God." This is the Hebrew *Shema* (Deut. 6:4). Why does James bring up this belief?

Read Deuteronomy 6:4-5. What is the primary duty of those who believe in one God? Why did Jesus connect the commandment to love God with the commandment to love one's neighbor? (See Mark 12:28-34.)

Meditate on James 2:21-26

In this section, James introduces two illustrations to establish his claim that faith and deeds go together. What is James's objective when he cites the story of Abraham's offer of Isaac? What does James mean when he says, "His faith was made complete by what he did?"

Read Romans 4:3 and Galatians 3:6. What seems to be the point Paul is making in these passages? Both Paul and James quote the same Scripture (Gen. 15:6). Based on your encounter with what James has said so far, how does James interpret and use Genesis 15:6 as a support for his argument? What does James mean by his statement in verse 24? How does this text change your understanding of the relationship between faith, deeds, and salvation?

Read the quote by William Barclay on page 42. What does Barclay say about a balanced Christian life? How do you respond to his comment?

In any well-proportioned life, there must be faith and works . . . If life is to be well-proportioned and fully effective in service and devotion, we must never think of it in terms of either or but always in terms of both and.
—William Barclay

Based on verse 24, how would you describe your life and relationship with God?

Read Joshua 2:1-21 and Hebrews 11:31. Evaluate James's statement about the righteousness of Rahab in light of these two texts. How does her story add light to the subject of connecting faith and actions?

Read the Hannah More quote. How would you relate this message of the interconnectedness of faith and deeds to a person who thinks faith alone is necessary for salvation? To a person who has no faith but plenty of good deeds?

If faith produces no works, I see that faith is not a living tree. Thus faith and works together grow, no separate life they never can know. They're soul and body, hand and heart. What God hath joined, let no man part.
—Hannah More

PRAYER ✝ ASK AND LISTEN

Seek the face of God. Ask, "Lord, what are You saying to us today?"

In this passage James invites us to have a balanced understanding of the relationship between faith and good works. Faith without works is dead; works without faith are also dead. Pray silently for God to show you the practical importance of faith and works in your life as a disciple of Jesus Christ. Ask Him to give you opportunities to put feet to your faith.

CONTEMPLATION ✝ REFLECT AND YIELD

How would you characterize your faith? Is it a living faith or a dead faith?

If your life as a disciple of Jesus Christ is preoccupied with either faith or works only, accept the challenge to yield to the voice of God speaking through James.

GROUP STUDY

- What is your definition of faith?

- What is your definition of deeds?

- Why does James say faith without actions cannot save a person?

- What is the difference between sharing one's faith and showing one's faith? Give an example of each.

- James uses the example of Abraham as a person whose faith and actions worked together. Can you think of other people whose lives have been an example of faith and action working together?

- Why is a living and active faith so important to our Christian life?

- Write down some specific ways you can exercise your faith this week.

LIVING WITH AN ENEMY
LISTENING FOR GOD THROUGH JAMES 3:1-12

Summary

All of us know the destructive and poisonous power of an un-controlled tongue. We daily witness strife and conflict in our human relationships caused by the words of a venom-laced tongue. In this lesson, James reminds us how this small organ in our body can cause big problems. This small part of our body has the power to set our whole life on a path of destruction. If uncontrolled, the tongue can spread havoc like wildfire.

Yet the tongue, if controlled, can set life on its proper course. How is it possible to control the tongue? James says this humanly impossible thing is indeed possible. The power to control the tongue does not rest in human capacity; it comes as a gift from God. With God's help, you can indeed have victory over this enemy within you.

PREPARATION ☦ FOCUS YOUR THOUGHTS

Do you speak often when you are in the company of others, feeling the need to be heard? If so, why?

What is your own assessment of your speech? If you could change one thing about your speech habit, what would it be?

READING ☦ HEAR THE WORD

James leads us through a conversation about the power of the tongue. Though it is a small organ, the tongue has tremendous power. James is not appealing for silence, but rather for speech that is controlled and beneficial to the whole community.

In this Scripture, you will encounter the following terms:

Teachers: Those entrusted with conveying the truth.
Stumble in many ways: Literally, we commit many sins.
Never at fault in what he says: One who has never sinned in his speech.
Keep . . . in check: To bridle.
Bits: Part of the bridle that keeps a horse under control.
Rudder: The person who controls this controls the ship.
A world of evil: The world of iniquity, as opposed to the world of truth and goodness.
God's likeness: Refers to humanity created in the image and likeness of God.

Read James 3:1-12, listening to what God will say to you in these powerful images.

MEDITATION ⚜ ENGAGE THE WORD

Meditate on James 3:1-2

James begins this section with the warning that teaching in the Christian community is a responsibility that should be undertaken with utmost seriousness. Read Acts 15:24, 18:24-26, Romans 2:17-29, 1 Timothy 1:6-7, 6:3-5, and 2 Timothy 4:3. What are the different types of teachers we find in these passages? What place did teachers have in early Christian faith? What was the greatest privilege of early Christian teachers?

What are some of the positive and negative influences teachers can have on their students? Why do you think James says teachers will be judged more strictly? What are the criteria by which teachers will be judged?

Read the quote from the Sayings of the Fathers. What might be the message of this ancient Jewish saying?

He who multiplies words multiplies sin.

—Sayings of the Fathers

In verse 2, James recognizes the universal problem of sin that affects all humanity. He also recognizes the reality that the most common sin is the sin caused by one's speech. He concludes that a person who has never been slipped up by his words is a perfect individual. However, the hypothetical nature of verse 2 shows the difficulty of attaining this virtue. Reread verse 2. What might James be saying about the relationship between perfection as a virtue and one's speech?

Meditate on James 3:3-6

Though the tongue is a small part of the human body, it has the greatest potential to be a positive influence upon the rest of the body. It can also lead to destructive and damaging consequences. How have you seen this play out in your own life?

James uses three illustrations in verses 3-5 (bits, a rudder, and a spark) to make his point. How do these illustrations clarify James's message?

Think of a time when you were cautious and controlled in your speech when tensions were developing in your relationship with someone. What was its outcome?

Why is it so difficult for most of us to control our tongue?

Read Proverbs 16:27, and relate its truth to verse 5.

An uncontrolled tongue not only corrupts the whole course of one's life, but it also wreaks havoc by setting one's life on fire. James says this fire comes from hell *(gehenna)*, which is Satan's dominion. It is possible that James is tracing the destructive potential of the tongue to the power of Satan. How does this concept add to your understanding of the necessity to control the tongue?

Read the quote by Phillip Brooks. Though James is not advocating silence, when does silence prove more effective than speech?

> A man who lives right, and is right, has more power in his silence than another has by his words.
>
> —Phillip Brooks

Meditate on James 3:7-12

Human beings have demonstrated the capacity to tame and control all creatures God created. However, they have failed to show their ability to control the poisonous power of the tongue. How do the metaphors in verses 11 and 12 illustrate the overall message of James?

James concludes this section with an appeal to Christians that this cannot be the way of life for them—Christians cannot be double-tongued. Both praise and cursing cannot come from the tongue of a Christian. How does that strong statement affect you?

Read the quote by Jesus. In what ways does Jesus' statement help us understand what James is saying?

> By their fruit you will recognize them. Do people pick grapes from thornbushes, or figs from thistles? Likewise every good tree bears good fruit, but a bad tree bears bad fruit. A good tree cannot bear bad fruit, and a bad tree cannot bear good fruit.
>
> —Jesus (Matt. 7:16-17)

James's discourse on the tongue is connected to his emphasis on perfect wisdom. (See James 1:5-8; 3:13—4:10.) Both of these passages deal with a double-minded person. (See 1:8 and 4:8.) What conclusion can you draw about the source of one's controlled tongue and pure speech?

If it is in our nature to have an unbridled tongue, how can we control our tongues—having only pure water proceeding from them? Where will we find the strength and ability to do this?

PRAYER ⚜ ASK AND LISTEN

Seek the face of God. Ask, "Lord, what are You saying to us today?"

James instructs us on the damaging effect of an uncontrolled tongue. James also instructs on the need for pure speech that flows out of a pure heart.

Pray silently, and ask God to speak to you as you reflect on this Scripture.

CONTEMPLATION 🕆 REFLECT AND YIELD

What did God reveal to you concerning your tongue? How do you respond to James's admonition in verse 10: "Out of the same mouth come praise and cursing. My brothers [and sisters], this should not be." Are you willing to seek God's strength to control your tongue?

GROUP STUDY

- Think of a time when you failed to control your tongue. What was the outcome?

- James uses the illustration of a small spark which can set a great forest on fire (v. 5). How can something so small as our tongue have so much power to cause harm?

- Why does the tongue have the ability to corrupt "the whole person" and "set the whole course of our life on fire" (v. 6)?

- Have you ever been guilty of praising God and cursing others (v. 9)?

- What are examples of the tongue being used for blessing?

- What are some of the ways God can help our mouths become sources of flowing fresh water?

- Our speech should build up and not destroy others. Describe a specific course of action you will take to be more disciplined in your speech. Make a commitment to be a good listener, and speak only words that are full of grace.

A GRACE-FILLED LIFE

LISTENING FOR GOD THROUGH
JAMES 3:13—4:10

Summary

There are two ways to live life. One option is to live in constant conflict with others, and the alternative is to live a life of peace and harmony with others. Conflict with others arises out of envy, selfish ambition, and a lack of humility. Lives lived in conflict are dictated by earthly wisdom, which promotes evil and disorder. Conversely, peace and harmony rule the lives of those who seek wisdom from above; such lives promote peace and righteousness in the world.

There is no middle ground, no third alternative or option, no place for a double life. James invites us to live a life filled with grace and wisdom that the world cannot offer. By the help of God's grace, you can indeed live a life filled with peace, humility, and mercy—a life that is the direct opposite of conflict and discord.

PREPARATION ✠ FOCUS YOUR THOUGHTS

How do you see your own relationships with others? Is there conflict and disharmony in your relationships? If so, what are you willing to do to bring peace and harmony with others?

READING ✠ HEAR THE WORD

James includes in his letter a collection of separate sayings, all focusing on the root causes of conflict in human relationships. He also instructs his readers regarding the actions they should take to bring peace and righteousness in the midst of chaos and disorder.

In this Scripture, you will encounter the following terms:

> *Wise and understanding:* The combination of the words *wise* and *understanding* is found in a number of places in the Old Testament. Using these terms James is addressing anyone who might pride himself as a teacher in the Church.
>
> *Humility:* A characteristic quality of teachers, stressed in the Jewish tradition.
>
> *Truth:* In this context, James may be referring to wisdom characterized by humility.
>
> *Unspiritual:* in this context the word *unspiritual* refers to that which is physical.
>
> *Peace-loving, considerate, submissive, full of mercy and good*

fruit, impartial and sincere: These all are characteristic qualities of Christian life. (See Gal. 5:22.)

Harvest of righteousness: The fruit-bearing result of living a godly life.

Desires: By this word, James means to draw our attention to the sinful and self-indulgent pleasures of our pre-Christ natures.

Grace: Though the word often means favor, here it may mean God's help.

Wash your hands . . . purify your hearts: A call not to external performance, but to inward transformation.

Thoughtfully and with spiritual ears listening for God's voice, read James 3:13—4:10.

MEDITATION ✟ ENGAGE THE WORD

Meditate on James 3:13-18

James reminds his readers that those who claim to have wisdom (those who claim to be teachers) need to show humility in their lives. What would be the outcome if good deeds are not done in a spirit of humility?

Read 1 Peter 2:12, and relate this verse to what James is saying in 3:13.

Read the quote from the Sayings of the Fathers addressed to

teachers. This Jewish saying refers to the Torah as the source of wisdom. What is the relationship between James's words and this Jewish saying about the virtue of teachers?

> Lessen your labor for worldly goods, and occupy yourself with Torah; be humble of spirit before all men.
> —Sayings of the Fathers

True wisdom produces two things: good works and humility. James contrasts the wisdom of this world with the wisdom from above to illustrate the interconnectedness of wisdom, good works, and humility. List the character traits of those who have the wisdom that is of this earth (vv. 14-16). What impact do these have on the community? List the character traits of those who have wisdom from above (vv. 17-18). What impact do these have on the community?

Based on verse 18, what is the ultimate responsibility of those who claim to be wise and understanding (teachers) in the Christian community?

Meditate on James 4:1-6

In this section, James turns his attention to the source of dissention and conflict within the Christian community. Desire, when it is not easily satisfied, leads to conflicts that affect relationships within the community.

Read Matthew 7:7-8, and relate these verses to James 4:3. How does James help us understand the teaching of Jesus? According to James, what kind of prayer does God not answer?

Read the quote by Garth Brooks. What is a prayer that you have prayed that was not answered? Are you now glad that your prayer was not answered?

> Sometimes the best prayers are the ones God does not answer. —Garth Brooks

Why do you think James addresses his audience as "adulterers?" How did James's audience prove to be friends of the world? How did friendship with the world impact their relationship with God? In what areas of your life do you find yourself in friendship with the world?

Verse 5 is difficult; consult other translations for different readings of this verse. The NIV seems to give attention to the human spirit. A number of other translations read this verse as referring to God's jealousy for His people. How does each possible interpretation of this passage apply to your life?

James concludes this section with the reminder that God gives grace, which is more than adequate to meet His divine requirement of humility.

Read the quote by John Selden. Why do you think people often talk about humility but seldom practice it?

> *Humility is a virtue all preach, none practice; and yet everybody is content to hear.* —John Selden

How does James contrast the proud and the humble in verse 6?

Meditate on James 4:7-10

There is only one way to deal with conflict and strife within the community of faith. What can one do to receive the gift of grace and the gift of wisdom?

James calls his audience double-minded. This seems to be James's favorite word for the spiritually unstable. Based on your reading of James 3:13—4:10, what causes double-mindedness among Christians?

Read 1 Peter 5:5-9. What similarities do you find between 1 Peter 5:5-9 and James 4:7-10? What do these two texts say about the practice of repentance in the early Christian community?

PRAYER ♱ ASK AND LISTEN

Seek the face of God. Ask, "Lord, what are You saying to us today?"

What are the things that cause you to be spiritually unstable? Pray silently and ask God to reveal the things that cause you to be double-minded.

CONTEMPLATION ☦ REFLECT AND YIELD

How would your relationship with others change if you received more grace from God?

How do you contribute to harmony and peace in your relationships? Are you ready to accept God's instructions to live a grace-filled life?

GROUP STUDY

- How does James relate humility to wisdom? According to James, what is the true test of humility?

- What connection does James see between unmet human desires and unanswered prayer?

- What difference does the grace of God make in your life?

- How does His grace equip and strengthen you to be a peacemaker?

- What specific actions do you take when you repent of sin?

- What is the response of God to those who humble themselves before Him?

- God calls us not only to live in peace with others, but to be peacemakers. He also calls us to live grace-filled lives, in friendship with Him. List the things you will commit to do to fulfill God's purpose for your life.

JUDGMENT DAY IS COMING

LISTENING FOR GOD THROUGH JAMES 4:11—5:6

SUMMARY

Love your neighbor as yourself. This is easier said than done. We may say we love our neighbor, but often our actions do not show it. We may say we love our neighbor, but often our neighbor is the subject of our slanderous conversations rather than the focus of our loving attention.

More often than not, we love ourselves more than we love our neighbor. This is evident in the way we are preoccupied with material wealth and worldly pleasures.

James tells his readers why they should not judge others. He calls them to live a life depending on God's plans for them, and he teaches them what to do if they are pursuing a life preoccupied with wealth and riches. These words of wisdom call for actions that will put you on the right track with God.

PREPARATION ⚜ FOCUS YOUR THOUGHTS

Do you have a tendency to pass judgment on others?

Do you take control of your life and set the agenda for your future? Do you live a self-indulgent life with no thought of the coming judgment of God?

What would you want to change in these areas?

READING ⚜ HEAR THE WORD

In this reading, you will find James's instructions on keeping the law of love. Ultimately, this will be the basis of the final judgment.

In this Scripture, you will encounter the following terms:

>*The law:* Most likely the royal law. (See James 2:8.)
>*The one who is able to save and destroy:* This refers to God as the final Judge and the one to whom people must make their appeal.
>*If the Lord wills:* This statement indicates one's dependence on God and an acknowledgement that human life is in the hands of God.
>*Hoarded wealth:* James may be using this phrase in an ironic way to mean storing up God's wrath.
>*Lord Almighty:* The Old Testament form, *Lord Sabaoth*

(The Lord of Hosts), depicts God as the Commander of a great heavenly army.

Innocent men: The poor who are righteous.

Read James 4:11—5:6, paying special attention to these phrases.

MEDITATION ⚜ ENGAGE THE WORD

Meditate on James 4:11-12

Slander has become a sickness that has affected our whole world. It spreads at epidemic pace particularly during election times. One cannot stand in line at the grocery store without observing headlines of tabloids that slander celebrities or politicians. James is concerned, in particular, with slander in the Church. What are the different ways by which Christians in the first century might have slandered other Christians? (For example, consider the Jewish-Gentile makeup of the Church. How would it have contributed to slander in the Church?)

James's concern for Christians is that they should keep the law of love. Those who pass judgment on others not only reject the call to love their neighbor, but they are also being critical of the law.

Read the quote from Jesus on page 64. How do you relate James's words to the words of Jesus?

> *For in the same way you judge others, you will be judged, and with the measure you use, it will be measured to you.*　　　　　—Jesus (Matt. 7:2)

Read Isaiah 33:22, and relate the prophet's words to what James says about God.

Meditate on James 4:13-17

What is the attitude reflected in the words James quotes in verse 13?

James is not very concerned with the issues of making business plans or money, despite the fact that trade and commerce were the primary livelihoods for many Christians in the first century. His concern is those who are arrogant and self-confident. Such arrogance almost always shows itself in one's capacity to control the events that lie ahead. How does this knowledge affect the plans you are making in your own life today?

Compare James 4:14b with Hosea 13:3. Hosea draws a similar analogy to describe the fate of the wicked. How do you respond to these analogies?

Though life is described elsewhere as transitory (see Ps. 90:5-6; Isa. 40:6-8), James may be focusing here on the fate of the arrogant. What is the basic attitude of those who say the words quoted in verse 15? How do you know when these words simply become a meaningless religious formula and not real expression of humility before God?

With this in mind, can you think of instances when you have talked about God and His involvement in your future, but went ahead and made plans for yourself without seeking God's direction?

James reminds Christians that sin is not only bad things that we have done, but also our failure to do that which we have been commanded to do. Read the quote by Mother Teresa, which puts this statement into vivid context. What are the frequently committed sins of omission in the Christian life based on this quote? Which ones have you committed by omitting?

> At the end of life we will not be judged by how many diplomas we have received, how much money we have made, how many great things we have done. We will be judged by "I was hungry and you fed me, I was naked and you clothed me, I was homeless and you took me in."
> —Mother Teresa

Meditate on James 5:1-6

James announces to his readers that the Day of Judgment has already come down upon the rich who hoard their wealth and oppress the poor. Compare James's reference to earthly treasure with Jesus' words in Matthew 6:19-20.

In the ancient culture, hoarding wealth was a sin against the community, because the wealthy were under obligation to give liberally to public and private needs. James uses words such as rotted, corroded, hoarded, etc. What might James be saying about wealth that is not shared with others?

Read the quote by John Wesley. How does this help you formulate a proper perspective on money and stewardship?

Earn all you can, save all you can, give all you can.
—John Wesley

James reminds readers that God will bring His righteous judgment on those who have accumulated wealth by exploiting those who worked for them. Withholding fair wages from laborers is an act of injustice. Read Leviticus 19:13. See how this law is expanded in Deuteronomy 24:14-15. What do these Old Testament laws say about withholding wages from a laborer? How do they still apply to contemporary life?

PRAYER ⚜ ASK AND LISTEN

Seek the face of God. Ask, "Lord, what are You saying to us today?"

The New Testament clearly teaches the truth that God's judgment is on all those who reject His call to love their neighbor. James instructs us not to pass judgment on others, not to be obsessed with our own life, and not to hoard wealth for our own pleasure. Pray silently, and wait for God to speak to you through this lesson.

CONTEMPLATION ⚜ REFLECT AND YIELD

What changes need to take place in your life, in light of God's Word through James? Are you willing to accept the challenges found in this lesson?

GROUP STUDY

- How do Christians slander other Christians today? Can you think of some examples?

- The Day of Judgment should not be the reason for righteous living. If you are in a situation where others are violating the law of love by slandering another person, what can you do about it?

- James warns those who slander and pass judgment on others that God alone is the only Judge of all humanity. Why does James say only God is able to judge?

- In what ways do you see oppression of the poor by the rich in our world?

- How should the Church respond when there is large-scale neglect and even exploitation of the poor in public and corporate economic policy?

- Think of a specific way you could share your wealth with others who need your help this week.

PATIENCE AND PRAYER
LISTENING FOR GOD THROUGH JAMES 5:7-20

SUMMARY

There is a huge scar on my stomach that reminds me every day that God intervened and saved me from a life-threatening infection when I was less than two months old. Doctors could provide no help. My parents told me the only thing they could do was pray and wait for God to heal me.

I believe in the power of prayer for healing, but I also believe we must wait patiently for God to carry out His will according to His good purposes.

James is a book on practical wisdom. In this last section of his book, James speaks on various issues that are important to your Christian life: waiting for God, maintaining integrity in speech, praying for the sick, confessing sin, and doing everything to bring home those who have gone astray from their Christian faith.

PREPARATION ✝ FOCUS YOUR THOUGHTS

What is your expectation when you pray for an urgent need? Are you willing to wait for God to respond in His time and according to His will?

READING ✝ HEAR THE WORD

James concludes his letter with some of his most practical instructions on Christlike living. He addresses issues of patience, swearing, prayer, healing, and seeking out the lost. In this Scripture, you will encounter the following terms:

> *The Lord's coming:* The Greek word *parousia* is the commonly used word in the New Testament for the Second Coming.
>
> *Elders:* A well-established order of ministry in the Early Church; elders were spiritually mature men appointed to give spiritual guidance to the congregation.
>
> *Anoint him with oil:* This means to symbolically set apart the sick person for God's special care and action.

Consider these phrases as you read James 5:7-20.

MEDITATION ✝ ENGAGE THE WORD

Meditate on James 5:7-11

What is your level of patience when you want to acquire

something? How about your level of patience with others who may be somewhat slow in their actions?

Patience is a virtue, but not many people have it. Psalmists often call their readers to wait for the Lord (Ps. 27:14; 40:1). Waiting is a sign of one's patience. However, we also find the righteous crying out, "How long, O LORD" (Ps. 13:1; Rev. 6:10)?

James admonishes his readers to wait patiently for the coming of the Lord—a much-anticipated event in the first century. Christians during this time believed they would be alive to see the coming of the Lord. How do you suppose this anticipation was heightened by the intensity of persecution they faced?

James calls Christians to imitate the farmer who waits patiently for the rains. Can you think of a time when you waited patiently for God to answer your prayer? Are there instances when you were impatient with God? How did your impatience impact your relationship with Him?

Read the quote by Barclay. What is the necessary ingredient for patience? How does knowing the character of God make it easier to wait for His answers to come?

> There will be moments in life when we think that God has forgotten, but if we cling to the remnants of faith, at the end of life we too shall see that God is very kind and very merciful.   —William Barclay

Patience will reveal not only the purpose of God for His people during their trials, but also prove that He is a compassionate and merciful God. How have you seen these character traits of God evidenced in your own life?

Meditate on James 5:12-18

Oath-taking is a serious matter, as it guarantees the integrity of one's speech. However, frequent oath-taking may become a way to avoid telling the truth. Consider how often some people say, "I swear!" after making a claim. How much credence do you put in the word of people who feel the need to add this phrase to their statements on a frequent basis?

Read the quote by Aeschylus. What is the emphasis of this quote?

> It is not the oath that makes us believe the man, but
> the man the oath.   —Aeschylus
>   (Fifth-century Greek writer)

Integrity of speech seems to be the alternative to oath-taking that James places before his readers. Where there is truthful speech, there is seldom any need for swearing. How does this knowledge affect the way you will speak in the future?

James concludes this section with instructions on prayer and healing. Why do you think James insists on involving the community of believers in prayer for healing? Why are some people in our day hesitant to ask for a public healing service? Why do they prefer anointing to be a private ritual?

James urges his audience to confess their sins (v. 16). What place does the confession of sin have in your life? Why does James think confession of sin is necessary? What kind of healing takes place as a result of confessing our sin?

Meditate on James 5:19-20

James ends his letter with a charge to seek out those who have gone astray and left the Christian faith. Read Matthew 18:10-14. How does this text clarify James's admonition?

Read the quote from Proverbs 10:12. It is likely that James has this proverb in mind. What might be the final word he is giving to his readers? How do you relate this final verse to James's previous instruction to fulfill the royal law?

> Hatred stirs up dissension, but love covers over all wrongs.   —Proverbs 10:12

PRAYER ⚓ ASK AND LISTEN

Seek the face of God. Ask, "Lord, what are You saying to us today?"

Is faith that leads to patience at work in your life? What about truthfulness in speech?

Pray silently, and ask God to fill you with His patience and pure speech.

CONTEMPLATION ⚜ REFLECT AND YIELD

How will these instructions of James change the way you live and practice your faith? Are you willing to follow God's instructions for you?

GROUP STUDY

- Why do so many people lack patience? How does the consumerism in our world contribute to this lack of patience?

- In what ways have you been involved in praying for others, especially during their illnesses? What effect did prayer for their healing have in your life?

- Can you think of reasons some people in modern society may associate illness with sin? Does Jesus say anything about this through words or actions?

- Why is it important to have a right relationship with God for people to recognize their physical, emotional, and spiritual health?

- Think of a person who is ill in your faith community. Set aside time to pray daily for the healing of that person. Take time to visit the person as well.

- How have the words of James had an influence on your relationship with God and others?

Ephesians
978-0-8341-5028-7

John
978-0-8341-5022-5

Philippians
978-0-8341-5021-8

Hebrews
978-0-8341-5024-9

1 & 2 Peter
978-0-8341-5025-6

Mark
978-0-8341-5015-7

Revelation
978-0-8341-5014-0

READ IT.
STUDY IT.
LIVE IT.

Life is busy. Take a moment to slow down and listen to God. Lectio Divina, Latin for *divine reading*, is a series of Bible studies that calls students to slow down, read Scripture, meditate on it, and prayerfully respond as they listen to God through His Word. This powerful series works great in small groups and individual Bible studies!

Order *Lectio Divina for Youth* Today!

www.ingramcontent.com/pod-product-compliance
Lightning Source LLC
Chambersburg PA
CBHW071929020426
42331CB00010B/2781